SGEULACHDAN NAN ÀIREAMHAN

THE NUMBER STORY

SMALL BOOK ONE

ENGLISH - SCOTTISH GAELIC

---

*Numbers Teach Children
Their Number Names*

written and illustrated by

MISS ANNA

Early Reader Edition of *The Number Story 1*
Bronze Medal Winner, 2016 Wishing Shelf Book Award

Copyright © 2018 by Jieeun Woo
Illustrations © Jieeun Woo

Cover by | Lumpy Publishing
Layout by | Lumpy Publishing
Translated by Ksandero Ksan Paŭel
Coloring by Jieeun Woo and Maria Mirabella

All rights reserved. No part of this book may be reproduced or transmitted in any form or by any means whatsoever, including photocopying, recording or by any information storage and retrieval system, without written permission from the publisher and/or author: missanna@missannabooks.com.

Library of Congress Control Number: 2018902040

Names: Miss Anna, author.
Title: Number story : numbers teach children their number names / Miss Anna.
Description: Portland, OR: Lumpy Publishing, 2018.
Identifiers: ISBN 978-0-9962164-4-9 | LCCN 2018902040
Summary: The pictures and rhymes present stories which introduce numbers 0-10.
Subjects: LCSH Numeration—English—Scottish Gaelic--Pictorial works--Juvenile literature. |
BISAC JUVENILE NONFICTION /
Languages: English—Scottish Gaelic
Classification: LCC QA141.3 .M57 2018 | DDC 513—dc23

Publisher: Lumpy Publishing
Website: www.missannabooks.com
Email: missanna@missannabooks.com

Paperback: ISBN 978-0-9962164-4-9
Printed in the U.S.A.   1 3 5 7 9 10 8 6 4 2

A bheil thu airson ainmean
nan àireamhan ionnsachadh?

It is very easy and a lot of fun!

Tha e gu math furasta is spòrsail!

Say-along our little jingle

Can an rann beag seo còmhla ruinn!

starting from Number One!

Tòisichidh sinn le Àireamh a h-Aon!

ONE looks like my one finger.

Tha AON coltach ri mo chorrag.

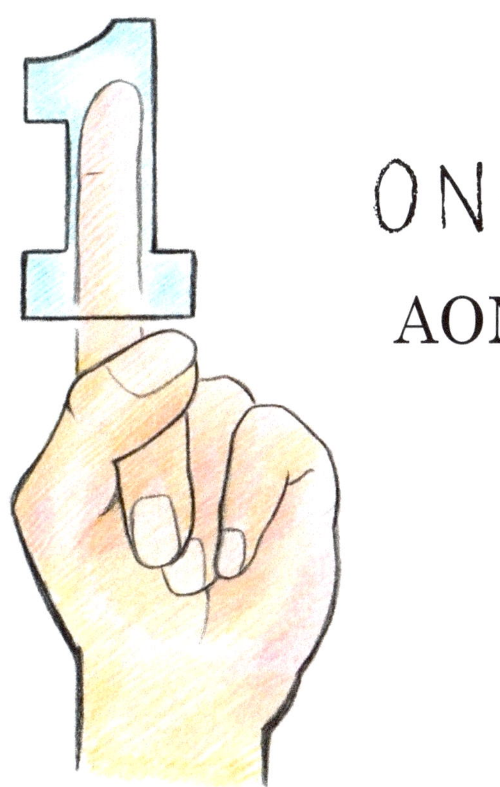

ONE!

AON!

2

TWO trails a tail.

DHÀ, tha earball air.

A TAIL! EARBALL!

3

THREE has bumps.

TRÌ, tha e cnapach.

Seall air na cnapan!

4

FOUR carries a sail.

CEITHIR, bata air seòl.

4
A SAIL!
SEÒL!

5
FIVE is a racing track.
CÒIG, tha e na thrac airson rèisean.

VROOM
BHROOM!
1

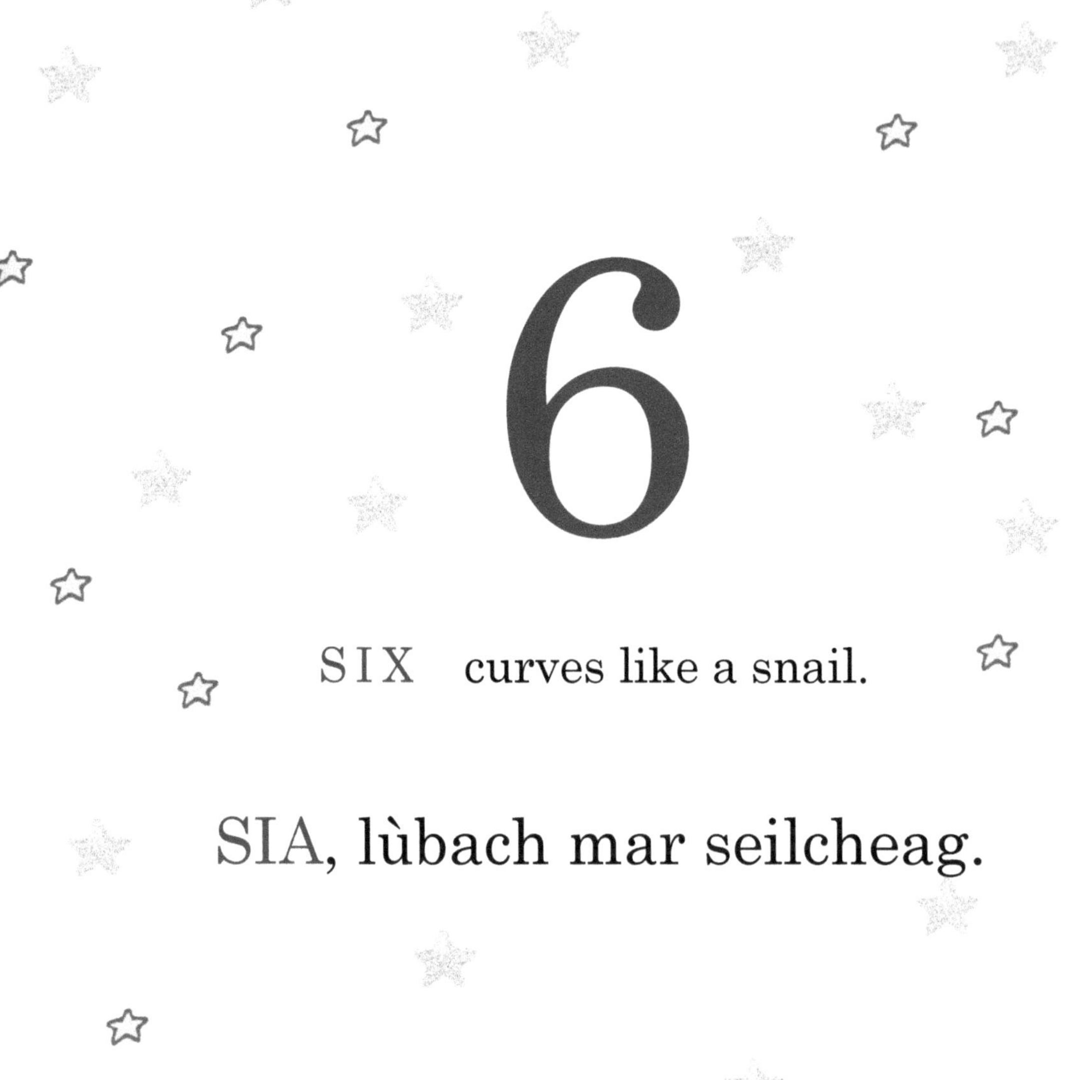

6

SIX   curves like a snail.

SIA, lùbach mar seilcheag.

A SNAIL! SEILCHEAG!

7

SEVEN has a sharp angle.

SEACHD, tha e biorach.

BE CAREFUL! IT'S SHARP!
BE FAICEALLACH! THA E BIORACH!

8

EIGHT   is a rollercoaster rails.

OCHD, tha e na *rollercoaster*.

YAY!
YIPPEE!

9

NINE   is a bubble on a stick.

NAOI, tha e na bhuilgean
air bata.

A BUBBLE!

BUILEAGAN!

10

TEN   is an eye of a whale.

DEICH, sùil aig muc-mhara.

WINK!
PRÌOB!
HELLO! HÀLLO!

And
Agus

0

ZERO   is an empty pail.

NEONI, tha e na bhucaid falamh.

IT'S EMPTY!
THA I FALAMH!

Thank you for playing with us today.

We had a lot of fun too!

Tapadh leat airson cluich còmhla ruinn an-diugh.

Bha tòrr spòrs againn cuideachd!

We are your Number friends,
Zero to Ten,
Who will be here for you~
Is sinne do chàirdean
Neoni gu Deich.
Bidh sinn daonnan an seo dhut!

Bye-bye now!
See you again soon!
Tioraidh an-dràsta!
Chì sinn a-rithist thu!

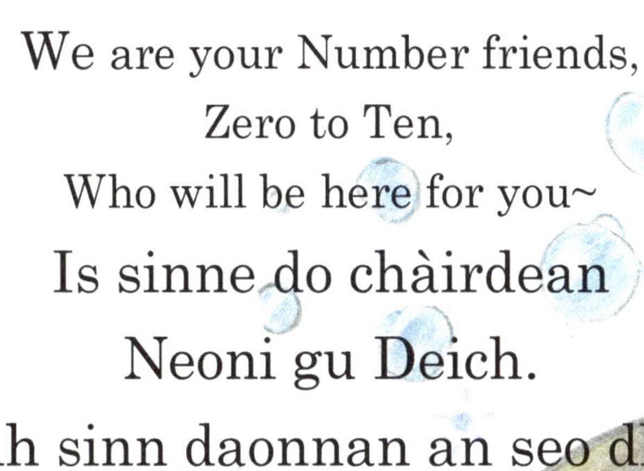

The Numbers are *SINGING* too!

To sing-a-long, look for Miss Anna Number Story
at your favorite music store like iTUNES.

MP3

Numbers 0-10
IDENTIFYING
& COUNTING

Numbers 11-20
& Ordinals
first, second, third...

Numbers 0-100
& Place Values
ones, tens, hundreds...

About Clocks
& Telling Time
hours, minutes, seconds

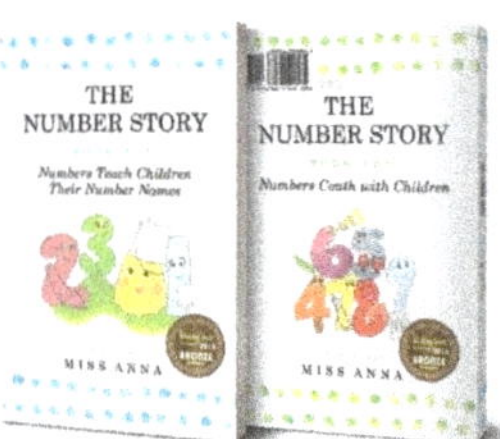

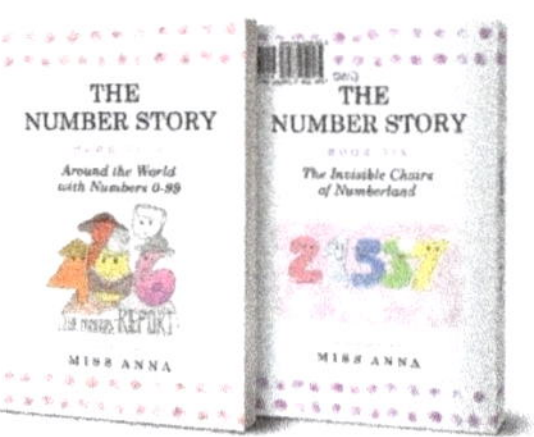

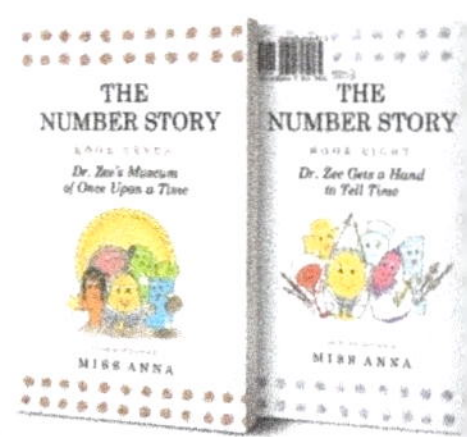

Number Story 1 & 2
isbn: 978-0-996216-48-7

Number Story 3 & 4
isbn: 978-1-945977-01-5

Number Story 5 & 6
isbn: 978-1-945977-06-0

Number Story 7 & 8
isbn: 978-1-949320-40-

For more Miss Anna books to love,
visit us at

www.missannabooks.com

Numbers are working hard all over the world!
Come Travel the World with Us!

www.ingramcontent.com/pod-product-compliance
Lightning Source LLC
Chambersburg PA
CBHW040859070726
47599CB00035B/2240